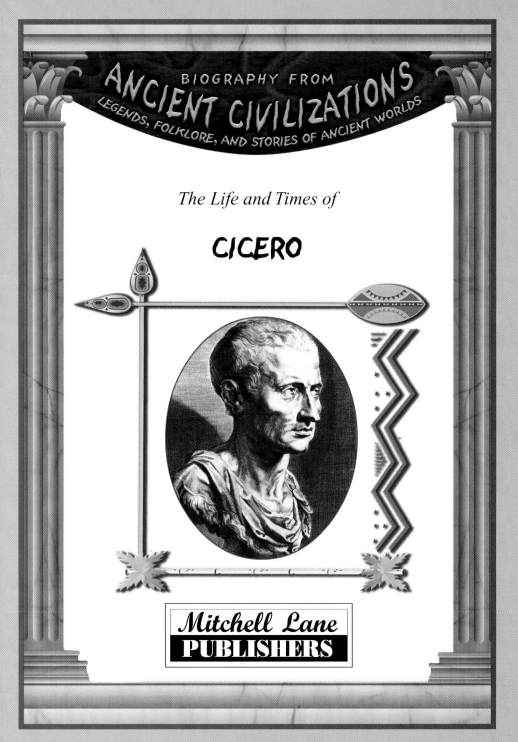

BIOGRAPHY FROM
ANCIENT CIVILIZATIONS
LEGENDS, FOLKLORE, AND STORIES OF ANCIENT WORLDS

The Life and Times of

CICERO

Mitchell Lane
PUBLISHERS

P.O. Box 196
Hockessin, Delaware 19707

BIOGRAPHY FROM ANCIENT CIVILIZATIONS
LEGENDS, FOLKLORE, AND STORIES OF ANCIENT WORLDS

Titles in the Series

The Life and Times of

BIOGRAPHY FROM
ANCIENT CIVILIZATIONS
LEGENDS, FOLKLORE, AND STORIES OF ANCIENT WORLDS

The Life and Times of

CICERO

Kathleen Tracy

Printing   1   2   3   4   5   6   7   8   9

Library of Congress Cataloging-in-Publication Data

Tracy, Kathleen.
    The life and times of Cicero / by Kathleen Tracy.
        p. cm. — (Biography from ancient civilizations)
    Includes bibliographical references and index.
    ISBN 1-58415-510-8 (library bound : alk. paper)
    1. Cicero, Marcus Tillius—Juvenile literature. 2. Statesmen—Rome—Biography —Juvenile literature. 3. Orators—Rome—Biography—Juvenile literature. 4. Rome—Politics and government—265–30 B.C.—Juvenile literature. I. Title. II. Series.
DG260.C5T73 2006
937'.05092—dc22
[B]   2005036803

ISBN-10: 1-58415-510-8   ISBN-13: 978-1-58415-510-2

ABOUT THE AUTHOR: Kathleen Tracy has been a journalist for over twenty years. Her writing has been featured in magazines including *The Toronto Star*'s "Star Week," *A Biography* magazine, *KidScreen* and *TV Times*. She is also the author of numerous biographies, including *The Boy Who Would Be King* (Dutton), *Jerry Seinfeld—The Entire Domain* (Carol Publishing), *Don Imus—America's Cowboy* (Carroll), *Mariano Guadalupe Vallejo*, *William Hewlett: Pioneer of the Computer Age*, and *The Watergate Scandal* (Mitchell Lane Publishers). In the Biography from Ancient Civilizations series for Mitchell Lane, she wrote *The Life and Times of Confucius* and *The Life and Times of Constantine*.

PHOTO CREDITS: Cover, pp. 1, 3—Hulton Archive/Getty Images; pp. 6, 18, 19—Barbara Marvis; pp. 8, 11, 31—Super Stock; pp. 9, 36—Corbis; p. 14—Wallace Collection; p. 20—Caen Basse; p. 22—Livius; pp. 28, 32, 36—Sharon Beck; p. 33—Time Life Pictures/Getty Images; p. 41—Getty Images.

PUBLISHER'S NOTE: This story is based on the author's extensive research, which she believes to be accurate. Documentation of such research is contained on page 47.

The internet sites referenced herein were active as of the publication date. Due to the fleeting nature of some web sites, we cannot guarantee they will all be active when you are reading this book.
    To reflect current usage, we have chosen to use the secular era designations BCE ("before the common era") and CE ("of the common era") instead of the traditional designations BC ("before Christ") and AD (*anno Domini*, "in the year of the Lord").

BIOGRAPHY FROM ANCIENT CIVILIZATIONS
LEGENDS, FOLKLORE, AND STORIES OF ANCIENT WORLDS

The Life and Times of

CICERO

        *For Your Information

Cicero was known in Roman times for his unmatched skill as a public speaker. He was also nearly as famous for his ambition and ego. Because he wanted to ensure his historical legacy, Cicero had most of his speeches published, which is how we know so much about his personal philosophies and political beliefs.

CHAPTER ONE

THE CATILINE CONSPIRACY

The Roman Senate was the scene of many historical events. It was where the leaders of the Republic would give flowery speeches and debate the best way to govern. It was also the scene of deceit, backstabbing, manipulation, conspiracies—and even murder.

One of the more dramatic controversies centered on a patrician named Catiline, who had served as governor of Africa in 67 BCE. Catiline considered himself an advocate for the common man and believed that all debts accrued under the reign of General Sulla should be canceled. Not surprisingly, the majority of aristocrats disagreed with that plan.

A year after he returned from Africa, Catiline was furious when he was prevented from running for consul, which in Rome was like a governor. During the Roman Republic there were two consuls who shared the job of ruling the country, similar to if the United States had two presidents with equal power. His candidacy was derailed by what turned out to be false accusations of misconduct in his previous office. Feeling cheated, Catiline allegedly devised a plot to murder the consuls. Whether he really intended to carry out the murders or was just letting off steam is unclear, but no attempts were ever made on the lives of the consuls. In 65 BCE, Catiline was ultimately acquitted of the charges of misconduct.

Once that was cleared up, Catiline was finally able to run for the consulship. Many of his supporters came to Rome to vote for him, and many believed he would easily win the position. But they under-estimated Cicero. In a blistering campaign speech, Cicero blasted Catiline as little more than a criminal. Catiline accused Cicero of playing dirty politics. For example, Cicero started wearing body armor, claiming Catiline was going to try to assassinate him in order to win the election.

Cicero won by a landslide. Catiline was so enraged by his defeat and by Cicero's depiction of him that this time he decided to overthrow Rome. The plan was for Catiline's followers in Rome to form a kind of sleeper cell, while Catiline enlisted others to organize an army for him outside of Rome. Part of their plan was to set Rome on fire during the Saturnalia, a weeks-long festival that honored Saturn, the god of agriculture. The chaos caused by the fire would make it easier to take over the city. Another of the tasks given the followers was to kill Cicero.

However, Cicero caught wind of the plot. One of Catiline's followers, a woman named Fulvia, was actually a double agent working for Cicero. Fulvia warned Cicero there was a threat against his life. When the would-be assassins showed up at his house, they were denied entrance and the plot was foiled.

It was believed that one of Catiline's secret followers was Marcus Crassus, considered one of Rome's richest men. He was the son of a former consul and desperately wanted to be considered a great politician. However, his best talent was in making money, not speeches. Although he never achieved his political aspirations, he was friends with Rome's most powerful men, including General Pompey, Julius Caesar, and Cicero.

Saturnalia was an important Roman holiday and festival. Celebrated in December at the time of the winter solstice to honor Saturn, the god of agriculture, gifts were exchanged and people enjoyed feasts and parties. When it was decided in the fourth century to celebrate Jesus' birthday, Pope Julius I declared the date as December 25. Some historians speculate he picked the date since pagans already observed it as a religious holiday, and it was a way of promoting the still-new religion of Christianity without alienating nonbelievers.

Late one night after the botched assassination attempt, Crassus showed up at Cicero's house. He showed Cicero several anonymous letters he had allegedly received warning Crassus and others to get out of Rome. The letters indicated there was going to be a massacre of those who remained behind.

Rather than leave, Cicero called an emergency meeting of the Senate and read the letters. It was there that others shared the rumors they had heard about Catiline organizing an army in the countryside outside of Rome with the help of a rebel commander named C. Manlius. The Senate ordered Roman troops to go confront Catiline's army. They also issued a *senatus consultum ultimum*, which was an official State of Emergency.

Known for his powerful public speaking abilities, Cicero stood before the Senate and made an impassioned speech against Catiline, who was present to hear the charges against him.

> Do you not feel that your plans are detected? Do you not see that your conspiracy is already arrested and rendered powerless by the knowledge which everyone possesses of it? . . . The Senate is aware of these things . . . and yet this man lives. He takes a part in the public deliberations; he is watching and marking down and checking off for slaughter every individual among us. And we . . . think that we are doing our duty to the republic if we keep out of the way of his frenzied attacks.
>
> You ought, O Catiline, long ago to have been led to execution by command of the consul. That destruction which you have been long plotting against us ought to have already fallen on your own head.[1]

Although Catiline bitterly renounced Cicero's speech, he knew his days in Rome were over. Late that night, he snuck out of the city, accompanied by 300 armed followers. He traveled north to join Manlius and his troops.

Hoping to improve their chances, one of Catiline's supporters contacted a delegation of Allobroges who happened to be in Rome. The Allobroges were a tribe in Gaul, which is now France. The follower suggested that the Allobroges, who were not happy being under Roman rule, start a revolt, which would further distract the Senate. Instead, the Allobroge delegation told an official, who in turn alerted Cicero.

Cicero decided to set up a sting operation. He needed proof that Catiline was planning to overthrow Rome and asked the Allobroges to help him get it.

Cicero speaks before the Roman Senate. His rousing speeches against Catiline helped earn him the reputation as one of Rome's greatest orators ever. However, his decision to execute members of the conspiracy without a trial would come back to haunt him.

The delegation pretended to go along with the planned revolt and gathered as much information as they could about Catiline, Manlius, and his army, and the rest of the conspirators. The plan worked, and many of Catiline's followers were arrested. But Catiline and Manlius, and their army, remained free.

Cicero faced another dilemma. As consul, what should he do with these conspirators? Although they had been caught with weapons and had tried to instigate the Allobroges, they had not actually committed a crime yet. Cicero thought a message should be sent to anyone thinking of trying to overthrow Rome. He favored immediate execution, but Roman law—based on a canon of rules known as the Twelve Tables—stated that no citizen could be executed without a public trial.

Julius Caesar was against execution. He believed the conspirators should be stripped of their belongings and imprisoned. After his speech, it appeared that the Senate would vote to do just that. But then Cato got up to speak. Cato was an extremely conservative politician who saw morality in black and white—in Cato's mind, there was no such thing as "extenuating circumstances." Anyone who even thought about raising arms against Rome was as much of a traitor as if he had burned the city down.

> Other crimes you may punish after they have been committed; but as to this, unless you prevent its commission, you will, when it has once taken effect, in vain appeal to justice. When the city is taken, no power is left to the vanquished. . . .
> We are beset by dangers on all sides; Catiline, with his army, is ready to devour us; while there are other enemies within the walls, and in the heart of the city; nor can any measures be taken, or any plans arranged, without their knowledge. . . . What I advise, then, is this: that since the state, by a treasonable combination of abandoned citizens, has been brought into the greatest peril . . . punishment be inflicted . . . as on men convicted of capital crimes.[2]

By the time Cato finished, the fate of the conspirators was sealed and Cicero's wish for execution was granted. It was a great victory for Cicero. An egotistical man, he considered himself to be no less than the savior of Rome. While his ego would be an important asset in his rise to being one of Rome's most famous orators and politicians, it would also frequently prove to be his downfall.

The Twelve Tables

Early in Rome's history, judges, called magistrates, wielded enormous power. The judges were always from the upper class, known as patricians, and acted independently. They often abused their power. Plebeians, or the common people, demanded a fairer system. In 450 BCE, five patricians and five plebeians were empowered to develop a code of Roman law that came to be known as the Twelve Tables.

Although simple, the rules outlined in the tablets covered a broad range of potential wrongdoing and specified both punishments and protections afforded Roman citizens. Prior to the Twelve Tables, there was no system for capital punishment; people could be—and often were— executed for minor crimes, such as being unable to repay a debt in a timely manner. The Twelve Tables outlawed such practices, stating that death sentences could be handed out only by a court. "Putting to death of any man, whosoever he might be, unconvicted is forbidden."[3]

However, the punishments for crimes were different depending upon whether the offender was an aristocrat, plebeian, or slave. For example, if an aristocrat or plebeian were caught stealing, he would be flogged and then be required to repay what he'd taken. But slaves caught stealing were flogged and then executed by being thrown off a cliff.

Each table covered a particular area, such as trial procedures, debt, a father's rights over his family, inheritance, property and land rights, personal injury, or capital punishment.

Laws always reflect the society they protect. Among some of the more unique laws in the Twelve Tables were:

- No burials were allowed within city limits
- Plebeians were forbidden to marry patricians
- Anyone convicted of stealing crops would be executed by clubbing
- Slander was punishable by death
- A witch could not cast a spell on another person
- Meetings could not be conducted at night

Perhaps the most important table was the last one, which stated, "Whatever the people had last ordained should be held as binding by law."[4] In other words, it reaffirmed the will of the populace would become law. This is why the Twelve Tables would ultimately serve as the foundation for all Western civil and criminal law.

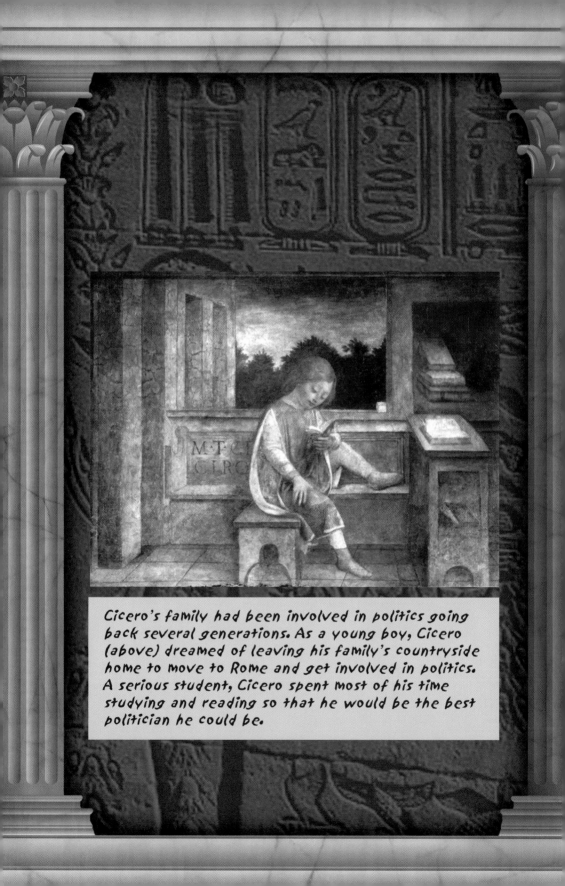

Cicero's family had been involved in politics going back several generations. As a young boy, Cicero (above) dreamed of leaving his family's countryside home to move to Rome and get involved in politics. A serious student, Cicero spent most of his time studying and reading so that he would be the best politician he could be.

CHAPTER
TWO

SETTING HIS SIGHTS

Marcus Tullius Cicero was born on January 3, 106 BCE. Two years later, his mother, Helvia, gave birth to another son, Quintus. Cicero and his brother grew up in Arpinum, a small town in the country about seventy miles—or three days' journey—southeast of Rome in the Italian countryside. The name Cicero means "chickpea." The family got the name Cicero because of an ancient ancestor who had a wart at the end of his nose.

Cicero was of Volscian decent. The Volsci were an Italian people who lived in the central part of the country. For many years, the Volsci and the Romans were bitter enemies and fought numerous wars. Finally, Rome conquered the Volsci, and eventually the Volsci were granted the rights of citizenship. Even so, Cicero and others who gained citizenship from Roman occupation rather than being born in Rome were often looked down upon by "true" Romans.

Cicero's family was aristocratic, or members of the local upper class. They owned land and grew crops, most likely olives and grapes. There is also some speculation that Cicero's family may have run a laundry business. At the time, washing clothes was considered a very undesirable job. Soap as we know it had not been invented, so cleaning clothes was time-consuming and messy. If in fact Cicero's family did laundry, he would not have wanted anyone to know about it after he moved to Rome as a young man.

While Cicero's uncle and grandfather were both involved in politics, his father, Marcus, was more interested in learning than debating. He suffered from frail health and seldom left the family estate, which was situated outside Arpinum in the rolling hillsides by the Liris River. The estate was a popular place for friends of the family to come and relax.

Always ambitious, as a young boy, Cicero dreamed of leaving the country for Rome. But when he got older, he grew to appreciate his hometown. "Whenever I can get out of Rome for a few days, especially during the summer, I come to this lovely and healthful spot. . . . This is really my country."[1]

Although many children of aristocrats were homeschooled by slaves or a tutor, Cicero and his brother went to an outside school. In addition to learning how to read and write, they were also taught arithmetic. Few people studied higher mathematics.

When he turned twelve, Cicero continued his education in the Roman version of high school. Unlike students of today who learn a wide variety of subjects, Cicero's education was limited to mostly literature and grammar. A few years later, Cicero's father decided it was time to expand his son's education. He sent Cicero to Rome, where the family also had a home. By that time, the young Cicero had already decided he wanted to pursue public life; specifically, to be a lawyer.

One of the most vital skills an attorney could have—then as now—was the ability to persuade people. As a teenager, Cicero went to study with an expert in public speaking called a rhetor, or rhetorician. Oration was so important that attending a school of rhetoric was practically mandatory for anyone wanting a career in public service. The best teachers were usually found in Greece, so studying abroad was an integral part of an upper-class young Roman man's education. Cicero, however, began his rhetoric studies with a private teacher in Rome after his father pulled some strings.

Suddenly, Cicero was being introduced to an entirely new world. He and Quintus would often visit a friend of the family named Lucius Licinius Crassus, a well-respected orator and lawyer. Crassus' house was located on the famed Palatine Hill, one of Rome's seven hills and where it is believed the city was actually founded. During Cicero's time, Palatine Hill was the Beverly Hills of Rome. Known for its spectacular views of the Forum and the Circus Maximus, and for shade trees, many of Rome's wealthiest citizens lived there. Years later, Roman emperors would take over the land for their personal palaces.

Cicero became close to Crassus' elderly father-in-law, Quintus Mucius Scaevola. The old lawyer took Cicero under his legal wings and tutored him on the art of advocacy. By all accounts, Cicero was a serious, dedicated student who considered recreation an unnecessary luxury. "The time which others spend in . . . taking holidays and attending games . . . proves in my case to have been taken up with . . . literary pursuits."[2]

However, there was one pastime he was passionate about. In his spare time, Cicero would attend trials held at the Forum and become spellbound by the inherent drama of watching people's lives hanging in the balance.

Although many elements of Roman trials are similar to modern court proceedings in the United States, there are some stark differences, too. Instead of just 12 jurors, there were anywhere from 30 to 60. The prosecutor and defense attorney each gave an opening statement. These were followed by statements from more lawyers because more than one attorney tried the case. Witnesses were called who would be cross-examined. Then the opposing counsels would get into a debate with each other. After that, there would be more speeches, and both sides would be allowed to present evidence.

Palatine Hill is one of the seven hills on which Rome was built. It is where the first ancient Romans settled. According to mythology, the founders of Rome were twins named Romulus and Remus. They were abandoned as infants but raised by a female wolf. When they grew up, they founded Rome on the hill where the wolf had saved them . During the Republic, Palatine Hill was home to Rome's wealthiest and most important citizens. (This photograph was taken in September 2005).

Finally, the jury would confer and decide on the verdict. The whole process would usually last several days. It became clear to Cicero that often the skill of the lawyer had more to do with the ultimate verdict than the evidence.

While studying with Scaevola at Crassus' house, Cicero met two other students who would play important roles in his life. The first was Julius Caesar, who was six years younger and related through marriage to Cicero and Quintus. The other was Titus Pomponius, also called Atticus, who would be Cicero's lifelong best friend.

In 91 BCE, the plebeians, or common people, elected Marcus Livius Drusus to be tribune. The tribune's job was to protect the plebeians' rights. Drusus' goal was to offer all Italians Roman citizenship. This idea was immediately shot down by the Senate. It wasn't a bad idea in and of itself, but the senators were afraid these new citizens would support Drusus and make him too powerful.

When one of the consuls criticized the Senate, Marcus Crassus gave an angry speech in the Senate's defense. Although the speech was well received—and made a lasting impression on Cicero—it also took its toll on the aging man. As soon as he finished, he became sick. Within days he contracted pneumonia and died.

The Roman Forum was the business and social center of Rome. Originally it was just a marketplace, but over the course of the Republic it was expanded to include the Senate and the courts, as well as several temples. The Forum was located in the valley between Palatine and Capitoline hills. (This photograph was taken in September 2005).

This is an artist's rendition of what Circus Maximus might have looked like. Circus Maximus was a gigantic sports arena that hosted chariot races. It also housed four stories of shops and vendors. It is estimated that it could seat at least 150,000 people.

When Drusus was assassinated a short time later, the hope that all Italians would be granted citizenship died with him. The Italians in the central and southern regions revolted in what would be known as the War of the Allies, or the Social War. Even though military service was expected of any Roman planning to move into public office, Cicero had not intended to enlist, preferring to concentrate on his studies. But the War of the Allies was too important a fight for him to ignore.

The young man who never played sports and had avoided physical exertion suddenly found himself a soldier. Cicero served on the staff of Gnaeus Pompeius Strabo, who led his troops to several important victories against the Italian Allies. It was during this time that Cicero met Strabo's son, Gnaeus Pompeius, or Pompey, who would one day be one of the most important men in Roman history. At the time, however, neither young man could know how intertwined their lives would become.

The conflict was bloody and bitter. Rather than face more revolts, the Senate reversed itself and agreed to extend citizenship to all Italians, as long as they remained loyal to Rome. Once the war was over, Cicero was able to go back to his studies and concentrate fully on becoming a lawyer—and earning the respect he so desperately desired.

The Roman Senate

Unlike the United States Senate, the Roman Senate did not propose legislation, although consuls could. The Roman Senate was a public forum for debating legislation. During the second and third centuries BCE, when Rome was rapidly expanding its empire across Europe, the Senate was responsible for declaring war, negotiating peace, and controlling Rome's finances. Perhaps most importantly, the Senate was also responsible for conducting criminal trials, supplying both the prosecution and the defense.

Although the original intent of the Senate was for its members to be made up of Rome's best citizens, in practice nearly all the senators were from a small group of influential aristocratic families and wealthy land-owners. Unless a senator was found guilty of some crime, membership to the Senate was for life. Nobody was elected a senator; a Roman man earned the honor by serving in any of a number of government positions.

For hundreds of years the Senate conducted business uneventfully, but by the time of Cicero, there was much drama surrounding it. Charges of corruption became commonplace, and the Empire had become so big that the Senate could no longer efficiently run it.

After an uprising that pitted wealthy aristocrats against middle-class citizens, two parties emerged in the Senate. On one side were the optimates, conservatives who resisted social change. On the other side were the populares, who believed Rome's wealth should be better distributed among all people, not just a handful of aristocrats.

Under the rule of Sulla, a general who initiated a civil war and ultimately took control of Rome around 90 BCE, the number of senators increased from 300 to 600. Fifty years later, Julius Caesar increased membership to 900. After Caesar's assassination, under the leadership of Octavian, many senators were labeled enemies of the state, and were either executed or run out of Italy. Octavian was named emperor, effectively ending the Roman Republic. He lowered the membership to 600. The new-look Senate was very nonconfrontational—and largely ineffectual. Although the Senate survived for the duration of the Empire, it never regained its authority and existed primarily as an homage to the former Republic.

Octavian

Lucius Cornelius Sulla, known simply as Sulla, was a ruthless Roman general who became dictator after engaging in a civil war with his rival, Gaius Marius. Once he gained power, he executed thousands of political enemies and supporters of Marius. His rule was marked by rampant corruption. Considered a tyrant, most of Sulla's policies—primarily aimed at increasing his power and diminishing the power of the Senate and plebeians—were overturned after his death.

CHAPTER
THREE

A RISING STAR

Once his military service was over, Cicero devoted himself completely to becoming the best advocate he could be. In addition to studying rhetoric, he also took acting lessons from a famous Roman actor, believing that theatricality was an important part of public speaking.

He finally began his career in 80 BCE, when he was in his mid-twenties. His first cases attracted little attention, which allowed him to gain experience and confidence in his abilities. He preferred defending rather than prosecuting, and his oratory skills earned many clients their freedom. Cicero didn't care whether the client was aristocrat or plebeian—he defended everyone with the same enthusiasm. He once had harsh words for a prominent orator who he said used "his great talents to injure men and not . . . to save them."[1]

That sense of justice earned Cicero a reputation for being a strong defender of the common man, which made him popular with plebeians. And his skill as an orator was gaining him respect among the aristocrats. Soon he would also be famous.

In 80 BCE, Cicero agreed to defend Sextus Roscius, who was accused of murdering his father. The elderly man, also called Roscius, had been killed while walking home from a dinner party. Although murdered in Rome, the older Roscius had a large estate in the country town of Ameria, and it was worth a lot of money.

Living on the estate was Sextus, who managed the property, his mother, two nephews—Titus Roscius Magnus and Titus Roscius Capito—along with several other relatives. It was well known that the elder Roscius had been on bad terms with the nephews.

At the time, Rome's ruler was a ruthless general named Sulla. After Sulla became dictator in 82 BCE, he published a list of "enemies of the state"—in other words, anyone who Sulla felt was a threat—and decreed they would be executed and their property seized. This was called proscription and was nothing more than a legal hit list.

Roscius' nephews sent word of the old man's death to Chrysogonus, who was a close friend of Sulla's. Even though the deadline for proscription had long passed, Roscius' name was suddenly added, after the fact, to the list. That meant most of his property would be forfeited to the state, which really meant it would be taken by Sulla's friend. The property was auctioned off. Of the thirteen farms on the estate, one of the nephews took three, while the other nephew, acting as Chrysogonus' representative, took the rest. Because it had been arranged for there to be no other bidders, they got the property for a minute fraction of its actual value.

Once the property was in his possession, one nephew kicked Sextus out even before he had finished making funeral arrangements for his father. When the locals of Ameria heard, they were appalled and set out to try to stop the nephews and restore rightful ownership to Sextus by appealing to Sulla himself. Chrysogonus intercepted their message.

Fearing for his life, Sextus fled to Rome, only to be accused by the nephews of murdering his father. Cicero agreed to defend him against the charge. Even though Sextus had an airtight alibi, Cicero knew this was a case in which the truth would be practically irrelevant. Sextus was actually locked in a power struggle with Chrysogonus, who wanted the son out of the way so that there would be no challenge to his ownership of the land.

This was the first murder trial since Sulla had come into power, and it was the talk of Rome. The proceedings attracted a huge audience of both plebeians and patricians. Also in the crowd were famous orators, because the Roscius family had many aristocratic friends. The excitement buzzing around the trial was like that in a theater. Cicero felt completely in his element and was ready to perform for the crowd.

Nearly everyone assumed Sextus Roscius would be found guilty—not because he was, but simply because it was no secret Chrysogonus was behind the trumped-up charges against the defendant.

The prosecutor was Erucius, a well-known orator who specialized in prosecutions. Because of Cicero's youth—he was only twenty-six—and because his previous cases had been rather mundane, Erucius paid little attention to the upstart lawyer. That would be his first mistake.

There was no question that Roscius had been in Ameria at the time of the murder, so the prosecution claimed he had hired assassins to kill his father. He proposed that since the son lived in the country and his father in Rome, they must have been on bad terms. The only reason the father would not have his son with him was because they were enemies. The argument was illogical at best. And although Erucius could not produce any evidence that this was actually true or that the son had hired anyone to kill his father, Erucius seemed unconcerned, believing the jury would simply go along with him.

Then Cicero stood to speak. He got everyone's attention by immediately bring up Chrysogonus' name. This took Erucius by surprise, and he suddenly started paying attention. Cicero wasn't worried about proving his client innocent—that was the easy part.

He knew the trick would be to make the jury feel it was their duty to acquit him and not be afraid of reprisals from Chrysogonus.

He pointed out the lack of orators willing to defend Roscius out of fear for their own well being. His implication was clear—that Sulla might seek revenge on behalf of his friend Chrysogonus if the trial did not go his way. Cicero did not boast of his own bravery; instead he said it was the fact he was so inconsequential, with no fame or fortune to worry about, that allowed him to freely defend Roscius.

Suddenly messengers began running in and out of the trial, no doubt carrying updates to Chrysogonus and Sulla. The tension grew as Cicero outlined the financial gain made by Chrysogonus and continued to persuade the jury to do the right thing. They did. Roscius was acquitted and overnight Cicero became famous—as much for his courage as his skills as an orator.

To Cicero, the real winner was law and reason. In his later years he would observe, "What is more divine, I will not say in man only, but in all heaven and earth, than reason? And reason, when it is full grown and perfected, is rightly called wisdom. Therefore, since there is nothing better than reason, and since it exists both in man and God, the first common possession of man and God is reason. . . . And since right reason is law, we must believe that men have law also in common with the gods."[2]

The Roscius triumph brought Cicero more clients than he could handle, and the workload eventually took its toll. After marrying a wealthy aristocrat named Terentia, he decided he needed a break.

Claiming ill health—and indeed he was plagued with stomach problems most of his life—Cicero took an extended vacation and traveled to Greece with a group of male friends. Oddly, he left his bride behind, but according to Anthony Everitt's *Cicero,* the couple was not particularly close in the early years of their marriage.

His time away from Rome would help Cicero regain his strength and strengthen his ambition.

Travel

In the twenty-first century, Italian vacationers can hop a plane to Greece, rent a car, and explore the country within a couple of weeks. But in Cicero's time, travel was far more complicated and time-consuming. It was also considered an integral part of any young man's education—that is, if he was from a wealthy family or showed unusual promise.

On average, the trip would take two years. In addition to studying with highly regarded teachers at one of Athens' universities, Romans would absorb the culture. They would visit historical locations and spend a great deal of time immersing themselves in the art and architecture of Athens. They would also travel to Egypt to explore Alexandria and the pyramids. Even then, taking a boat ride down the Nile was a popular attraction. Next, they would sail over to Asia Minor, what is now Turkey, and visit the ruins of Troy. The area was also famous for its spas, for which Romans had a particular fondness.

Ruins of Troy

Ironically, traveling to Greece was far safer than traveling through Italy or even just the outskirts of Rome. While the Roman system of roads was excellent, personal safety remained a major concern. Out in the country, bandits stalked the roads, hoping to come across someone foolhardy enough to be traveling alone. Aristocrats typically traveled with a posse of slaves and armed bodyguards, but those unable to afford such protections were frequently robbed and killed. People took road trips—by horse—only out of necessity, such as soldiers or politicians on official business or students trying to make their way to Greece to attend one of its universities. Pleasure trips by foot were simply not done.

Most Romans preferred traveling by ship. A short boat ride from Rome down the Tiber was Ostia, a vibrant port city that received ships from all across the Mediterranean and boasted markets selling goods of all kinds. After a day of shopping, the traveler could set sail for Greece. Barring bad weather, he would arrive in Athens in just four days.

ITALY

★Rome

Mediterranean
Sea

GREECE

Athens
★

Sicily

● Syracuse

Map not authoritative

The Greeks first started colonizing Sicily and the
southern end of modern Italy around 800 BCE. Even
during the Republic, most Sicilians spoke Greek,
not Latin. Over time, the Sicilian city of Syracuse
became an important port city. But Sicily was often
at odds with Rome and was the site of several slave
rebellions. The great mathematician Archimedes—who
devised integral calculus—was born in Syracuse.

CHAPTER
FOUR

POLITICAL ASPIRATIONS

While in Greece, Cicero studied philosophy in Athens. He fell in love with the ancient city and all its history. For a while, he seriously considered settling in Athens permanently, but after news of Sulla's death reached Greece in 78 BCE, Cicero decided to continue his education. He spent a year in Rhodes tutored by the best rhetoric teachers in the known world.

When he returned to Rome in 77 BCE, Cicero was healthy and strong and immediately set about to reestablish his legal career. He was also ready to pursue his political aspirations and mounted his first campaign for office. Because of the goodwill he had sown during his early days as a lawyer, and with the help of friends and hometown supporters, he was elected quaestor for Western Sicily in 75 BCE. Although the quaestor was the low man on the political totem pole, it was an important job. His duties were to administer the region's financial affairs, such as collecting taxes or purchasing extra crops if necessary.

Since wives were not permitted to accompany their husbands on official business, Terentia was again left in Rome—along with their young daughter, Tullia—while Cicero traveled to Sicily. When he wasn't working, Cicero spent his days absorbing Sicilian culture. He'd eat his lunch at local parks and plazas, cultivating goodwill by meeting as many people as he could, and accept invitations to dinner, where he could engage in lively conversation and debate. He was so respected that he was asked to prosecute the former governor of Sicily for extortion, which is using one's position of power to get money or something of value from someone. Cicero argued such a strong case that the governor chose not to fight the charges and voluntarily left the country.

When his term was over, Cicero returned to Rome with an even stronger reputation and resumed his legal practice. After breakfast, he would spend the morning working, then he'd meet with clients or go to the Forum to try a case or sit in on other trials. The evenings were usually spent dining with associates, and then he would return home to work late into the night. Although he adored his daughter and by all accounts grew close to his wife, the law remained Cicero's primary passion.

In 69 BCE, Cicero was elected aedile, which was an official in charge of maintaining temples and other public buildings and regulating public festivals. Three years later, he was voted in as one of eight praetors, which were comparable to judges. Praetors were assigned six bodyguards and were allowed to wear purple togas. During this time Cicero first publicly showed support for Pompey, who was considered one of Rome's greatest generals.

Pompey was born the same year as Cicero, 106 BCE, on September 29. The two had met during the War of the Allies when they had served with Pompey's father, Strabo. Pompey quickly earned a reputation as a skilled soldier, and after several victorious campaigns in Spain and leading the decisive battle against Spartacus and his followers, Pompey was hailed a hero. Despite his lack of administrative or political experience, Pompey was elected consul in 71 BCE at the age of thirty-five.

Four years later, Pompey was given the Herculean task of ridding the Mediterranean of pirates. In just a few months, he had driven the

Gnaeus Pompeius Strabo overcame humble beginnings to become one of Rome's most respected generals. He was elected consul, and during his reign the Italians in central Italy revolted over being denied Roman citizenship. Strabo led his troops and helped Rome with the War of the Allies. Despite his fame during Roman times, today Strabo is most famous for being the father of Pompey the Great.

pirates out and firmly established himself as Rome's leading military leader. His next assignment was to secure large sections of the Middle East, including Jerusalem. Once again, Pompey returned to Rome a hero. He was very upset when the Senate kept delaying giving his soldiers the land they had been promised in payment for their military victories.

Seeing an opportunity, Julius Caesar convinced Pompey and Crassus, who had served as consul in 70 BCE along with Pompey, to form an alliance, the First Triumvirate. They also asked Cicero to join forces with them, but he refused. After Pompey and Crassus helped Caesar win the consulship in 59 BCE, Caesar in turn saw to it that Pompey's men got the land they had been promised. For all intents and purposes, the three men were the unofficial leaders of Rome. Many in the Senate were very unhappy with this arrangement.

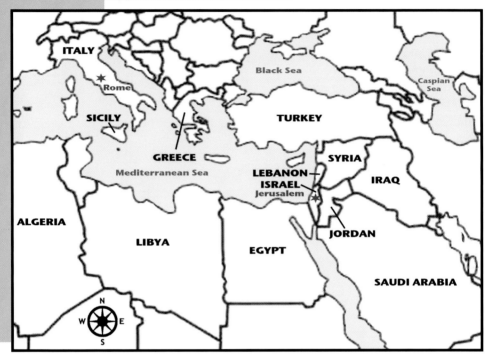

Among Pompey's more important military achievements was to conquer areas in the Middle East, including Jerusalem and what is now Syria, and put them under Roman rule.

Cicero would soon wish he hadn't rebuffed his powerful peers. Back in 62 BCE, a man named Publius Clodius Pulcher was caught sneaking into a religious ceremony that was strictly for women only. Word got out that Clodius had disguised himself as a woman in order to have a secret rendezvous with Pompeia, Julius Caesar's wife, at whose house the rites were being held. To this day nobody is sure whether or not Clodius was truly romantically involved with Pompeia, but Caesar ultimately divorced her anyway.

Clodius was charged with sacrilege and ordered to stand trial. His defense was to claim mistaken identity, saying he was ninety miles outside of Rome when the incident occurred. Cicero broke Clodius'

Julius Caesar possessed one of the most brilliant military minds in history. His conquests helped the Roman Republic spread its influence all the way to the Atlantic Ocean. He was also a masterful politician. After being named dictator, he instituted social and political reforms that greatly benefited the average Roman citizen.

alibi and presented evidence that proved he indeed had been seen in Rome just hours before sneaking into the ritual. Even though Clodius was able to bribe enough jurors to be acquitted, he swore one day he would get even with Cicero.

In 59 BCE, Clodius arranged to be adopted by a plebeian. That allowed him to run for the position of tribune; tribunes were the plebeian representatives in the Senate. He was elected, and a year later he got legislation passed that stated anyone who had executed a Roman without benefit of a trial should be exiled. Everyone knew the law was aimed directly at Cicero, who had carried out the executions of Catiline's men without putting them on trial first.

Cicero appealed to Pompey for help. When Pompey declined, Cicero was forced into exile.

In his biography of Cicero, nineteenth-century American politician Hannis Taylor describes the orator's departure from Rome.

> It was late in March when he left Rome, accompanied beyond the walls by tearful friends who assured him that he would soon be recalled. On the same day Clodius presented a bill in the assembly . . . providing that no one should receive [Cicero] in his house within five hundred miles of Italy. . . . It was further enacted that if he should be seen within the forbidden limits, he, with all who gave him shelter, might be killed with impunity. After being branded as a traitor to the commonwealth, his great mansion on the Palatine was given to the flames, and soon afterward his Formian and Tusculan villas were sacked and laid waste.[1]

During his exile, Cicero wrote long letters to his wife in which his upset is obvious, as is his concern for Terentia. "In a word, if you have any affection for me, let not your anxiety upon my account injure your health. . . . Believe me, you are the perpetual subject of my waking and sleeping thoughts. . . . I know not whom to write to, unless to those who first write to me, or whom you particularly mention in your letters. . . . Let me hear from you both as often as possible, particularly if there should be any fairer prospect of my return. Farewell, ye dearest objects of my most tender affection, Farewell!"[2]

Eventually, Pompey had a change of heart. With the agreement of the Senate, he recalled Cicero to Rome and officially ended his exile. In addition, the Senate awarded him damages and had his house and villas rebuilt.

Although he was happily settled back in Rome, Cicero was less politically active than prior to his exile. He spent much of his time writing essays and books on politics and rhetoric, such as *De oratore* and *De re publica*. But soon he would be drawn back into the political spotlight—a reemergence that would have fatal consequences.

Roman Meals

The kind of food Romans ate and the way they ate them depended in large part on how wealthy they were. Like today, Romans looked forward to three meals a day, and dinner parties were a popular social pastime for the aristocratic classes.

Here is a typical Roman menu:

Breakfast—Romans started their day very early, usually right after dawn.

Plebeians: Bread, either dry or dipped in wine. Occasionally if available, the bread was topped with olives, cheese, or raisins. For those out of work and unable to afford a decent breakfast, the government handed out bread every morning. Ironically, a lot of employed Romans would also grab some bread to eat on the way to work.

Patricians: Fruits sweetened with honey, bread, and fresh vegetables. Breakfast was cooked and served by slaves, who also cut the food into bite-sized pieces. Although Romans had spoons, they did not use knives or forks, so they frequently ate with their fingers. An aristocrat boy might also stop by a bakery on the way to school to buy a pancake.

Lunch—Because their workdays started early, lunchtime was typically before noon, around 11:00 A.M.

Plebeians: More bread with occasional cheese and olives.

Patricians: Cold meats left over from the previous night's dinner, along with nuts, salad, bread, and cheese.

Siesta—After lunch everyone, plebeian and patrician alike, would take a midday rest. During the sultry days of summer, most people actually took naps, leaving the stores closed and the streets practically deserted.

Dinner—The one hot meal in a Roman's day was dinner.

Plebeians: Vegetable stew and, when affordable, cooked fish. Because of the cost, meat was a rare treat. However, through the government welfare system, tokens were distributed that could be redeemed for various foodstuffs, including meat on special holidays.

Patricians: More than a meal for wealthy Romans, dinner was frequently a festive social event. Typically, men ate together; the women and children ate in another room. While reclining on cushions, men enjoyed a feast of various cooked meats, cheeses, and wines. Men's dinner parties often featured entertainment such as plays or dancing girls.

BULGARIA

Black Sea

RUSSIA

GEORGIA

GREECE

ARMENIA

AZER.

TURKEY

IRAN

Cilicia

IRAQ

SYRIA

Mediterrean Sea

LEBANON

0   100   200 mi
0   100 200 km

Cicero served as proconsul in Cilicia from 51 to 50 BCE. The area was originally part of the Hittite empire. The Hittites were an Indo-European people who settled in the region of modern-day Turkey in the second millennium BCE.

CHAPTER
FIVE

CIVIL WAR

In 55 BCE, Pompey and Crassus were again elected consuls. But after Crassus was killed in battle two years later, the Senate named Pompey sole consul in 52 BCE. He used his power to clean up the political corruption and lawlessness that was running rampant in Rome. Because there was a shortage of qualified officials to serve as governors in Rome's provinces, Cicero was called into service. In 51 BCE he was sent to Cilicia, a province located in what today is Turkey. By all accounts he was an honest governor, refusing to accept bribes and prosecuting criminal gangs. But he missed Rome and his family and was relieved when he was finally able to return home.

When he arrived in 49 BCE, Cicero was horrified to discover that the republic was on the verge of a civil war, with Pompey pitted against Caesar. Cicero had to decide which man to side with, and eventually chose Pompey.

In a letter written to his friend Tiro, Cicero noted, "I find myself surrounded with the flames of a civil war. . . . My friend Caesar had written a very warm and menacing letter to the senate. He had the boldness, notwithstanding their express prohibition, to continue at the head of his army and in the government of his province. . . . And never, in truth, were our liberties in more imminent danger. . . . We are raising forces with all possible diligence, under the authority and with the assistance of Pompey: who now begins, somewhat too late I fear, to be apprehensive of Caesar's power."[1]

Cicero had good reason to worry. Between Caesar's military skills and some misjudgments on Pompey's part, Caesar won the war. Pompey was assassinated while in Egypt, and it was reported that Caesar cried when he heard the news that his former best friend had been murdered. Caesar had the assassin executed and urged the Senate to honor Pompey by naming him a god.

Now Rome's undisputed leader, Caesar did not hold Cicero's decision to side with Pompey against him and gave him an official pardon. Depending on the source, Caesar was either a ruthless tyrant or a farsighted reformer. He was named dictator for life and immediately set out to reform Rome's government, which had been weakened by years of corruption and scandal.

Cicero's personal life was also in upheaval. According to Plutarch's biography of him, Cicero was not happy with the debt his wife had racked up and with her disinterest in philosophy and law. After thirty years of marriage, he divorced Terentia and soon after married a much younger woman named Publilia. That marriage ended after only a couple of months, after which Cicero decided to remain single and devote himself to his work.

While Cicero didn't seem particularly distressed to lose a wife, he was inconsolable when his daughter Tullia died during childbirth in 45 BCE. It was the biggest heartbreak of Cicero's life, and by most accounts was a tragedy from which he never fully recovered.

Meanwhile, Caesar continued his reforms, including changing the calendar, earning the love of the average Roman, and gaining the increasing distrust of many senators, who worried that Caesar's ultimate plan was to name himself emperor. In hopes of saving the

Republic, a group led by his friend Marcus Brutus assassinated Caesar in the Senate on March 15, called the Ides of March, in 44 BCE.

Caesar's death resulted in a power struggle between Caesar's nephew Octavian and Marc Antony, who had been Caesar's right-hand man. Viewing that Marc Antony was a "mad man," Cicero attacked Antony in a series of 14 speeches called the Philippics, in which he urged the Senate to declare Antony a public enemy and to throw their support behind Octavian. "O Romans . . . the foundations have been laid for future actions. For the senate has no longer been content with styling Antonius [Antony] an enemy in words, but it has shown by actions that it thinks him one. And now I am much more elated still,

Marc Antony was Caesar's loyal second in command as well as his cousin. At Caesar's funeral, Antony spoke forcefully against those who had conspired with the assassins to kill Caesar. He so riled the public that the assassins had to flee Rome in fear for their lives.

because you too with such great unanimity and with such a clamor have sanctioned our declaration that he is an enemy."[2]

Unfortunately for Cicero, Octavian and Antony realized it was in their mutual interest to join forces, so along with a politician named Marcus Lepidus, they formed the Second Triumvirate. Once the alliance was signed into law, the three men compiled lists of their political enemies for a proscription. The first name on Antony's list was Cicero, along with Cicero's brother, Quintus. Although Octavian tried to intervene and save Cicero, he ultimately gave in to Antony's wishes.

When Cicero and Quintus heard about the proscription, they made plans to flee to Greece. Before he could get away, Cicero was tracked down by two of Antony's henchmen on December 7, 43 BCE. Plutarch describes his final minutes:

> Cicero . . . commanded his servants to set down the litter; and stroking his chin, as he used to do, with his left hand, he looked steadfastly upon his murderers, his person covered with dust, his beard and hair untrimmed, and his face worn with his troubles. . . . And thus was he murdered, stretching forth his neck out of the litter, being now in his sixty-fourth year. Herennius cut off his head, and, by Antony's command, his hands also, by which his Philippics were written.[3]

As a final insult, Antony displayed Cicero's head and hands publicly at the Forum. About twelve years later, Antony would come to his own inglorious end. In 33 BCE the Second Triumvirate dissolved after Octavian and Antony had a disagreement that resulted in yet another civil war. After Octavian's army defeated Antony's, Antony committed suicide in Egypt.

In 27 BCE, Octavian was named Augustus Caesar, marking the official end of the Republic. Plutarch tells the story of Octavian visiting his grandson. "The boy had a book of Cicero's in his hands

Augustus Caesar was the first Roman emperor. Called Octavian, he was the great-nephew of Julius Caesar, who named Octavian his heir in his will. In 32 BCE, Octavian declared war against Marc Antony. His victory was quick and decisive. After Antony and his lover, Cleopatra, committed suicide, Octavian was named emperor. He ruled for over forty years, and under his leadership, Rome enjoyed peace and unequaled prosperity.

and, terrified of his grandfather, tried to hide it under his cloak. Caesar noticed this and, after taking the book from him, stood there and read a great part of it. He then handed it back to the young man with the words: 'A learned man, my child, a learned man and a lover of his country.' "[4]

During his life, Cicero was never given the level of respect he so desperately wanted from his contemporaries. However, in the centuries after his death he became recognized as one of the great ancient thinkers who through his writings brought the final years of the Roman Republic to vibrant life for all the generations that followed.

FYI
For Your Info

The Roman Calendar

While Julius Caesar is mostly remembered as a great general and a controversial politician, one of his most enduring legacies is still part of modern culture—the Julian calendar.

Originally, the Roman calendar had only 355 days. Every other year, 22 or 23 days would be added to keep the calendar synchronized with the solar year.

Caesar introduced a new calendar on January 1, 45 BCE. This new system had an average of 365 1/4 days, just as our calendars do today. To keep the calendar in line with the solar year, an extra day was added every four years between February 23 and 24.

The Romans divided each day into 24 hours as we do, but their days were counted from sunrise to sunrise. Every day had 12 hours of daytime and 12 hours of night. To match the clock with the sun, the number of minutes in each hour varied. During the summer, when the days were longer, each daylight hour had up to 76 minutes. In the dead of winter, the daylight hours may have been as short as 44 minutes. The only two days of the year that had 60-minute hours were the equinoxes, which were the first days of autumn and spring.

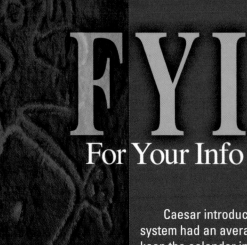

1	Kalendis	Kalendis	Kalendis	Kalendis
2	postridie Kalendas a.d. IV Nonas	postridie Kalendas a.d. IV Nonas	postridie Kalendas a.d. IV Nonas	postridie Kalendas a.d. VI Nonas
3	a.d. III Nonas	a.d. III Nonas	a.d. III Nonas	a.d. V Nonas
4	pridie Nonas	pridie Nonas	pridie Nonas	a.d. IV Nonas
5	Nonis	Nonis	Nonis	a.d. III Nonas
6	postridie Nonas a.d. VIII Idus	postridie Nonas a.d. VIII Idus	postridie Nonas a.d. VIII Idus	pridie Nonas
7	a.d. VII Idus	a.d. VII Idus	a.d. VII Idus	Nonis
8	a.d. VI Idus	a.d. VI Idus	a.d. VI Idus	postridie Nonas a.d. VIII Idus
9	a.d. V Idus	a.d. V Idus	a.d. V Idus	a.d. VII Idus
10	a.d. IV Idus	a.d. IV Idus	a.d. IV Idus	a.d. VI Idus
11	a.d. III Idus	a.d. III Idus	a.d. III Idus	a.d. V Idus
12	pridie Idus	pridie Idus	pridie Idus	a.d. IV Idus
13	Idibus	Idibus	Idibus	a.d. III Idus
14	postridie Idus a.d. XIX Kalendas	postridie Idus a.d. XVI Kalendas	postridie Idus a.d. XVIII Kalendas	pridie Idus
15	a.d. XVIII Kalendas	a.d. XV Kalendas	a.d. XVII Kalendas	Idibus
16	a.d. XVII Kalendas	a.d. XIV Kalendas	a.d. XVI Kalendas	postridie Idus a.d. XVII Kalendas
17	a.d. XVI Kalendas	a.d. XIII Kalendas	a.d. XV Kalendas	a.d. XVI Kalendas
18	a.d. XV Kalendas	a.d. XII Kalendas	a.d. XIV Kalendas	a.d. XV Kalendas
19	a.d. XIV Kalendas	a.d. XI Kalendas	a.d. XIII Kalendas	a.d. XIV Kalendas
20	a.d. XIII Kalendas	a.d. X Kalendas	a.d. XII Kalendas	a.d. XIII Kalendas
21	a.d. XII Kalendas	a.d. IX Kalendas	a.d. XI Kalendas	a.d. XII Kalendas
22	a.d. XI Kalendas	a.d. VIII Kalendas	a.d. X Kalendas	a.d. XI Kalendas
23	a.d. X Kalendas	a.d. VII Kalendas	a.d. IX Kalendas	a.d. X Kalendas
24	a.d. IX Kalendas	a.d. VI Kalendas	a.d. VIII Kalendas	a.d. IX Kalendas
25	a.d. VIII Kalendas	a.d. V Kalendas	a.d. VII Kalendas	a.d. VIII Kalendas
26	a.d. VII Kalendas	a.d. IV Kalendas	a.d. VI Kalendas	a.d. VII Kalendas
27	a.d. VI Kalendas	a.d. III Kalendas	a.d. V Kalendas	a.d. VI Kalendas
28	a.d. V Kalendas	pridie Kalendas	a.d. IV Kalendas	a.d. V Kalendas
29	a.d. IV Kalendas		a.d. III Kalendas	a.d. IV Kalendas
30	a.d. III Kalendas		pridie Kalendas	a.d. III Kalendas
31	pridie Kalendas			pridie Kalendas

The most complicated part of the Roman calendar was the naming system for days. Instead of having individual names for seven different days, the Romans named only three days. The first day of the month was called the Kalends, from the word *Kalendrium*, Latin for "account book." In Roman times, the first day of the month was when bills were due to be paid, so it made sense to name the day after something related to that. *Kalends* is also where we get the word *calendar*. The second important day was Nones, which was either the 7th or 5th day, depending on the month. The third named day was the Ides, which fell either on the 13th or 15th. All the other days were described in relation to those three.

The most infamous date in Roman history is the Ides of March. On that day in 44 BCE, Julius Caesar was assassinated in the Roman Senate.

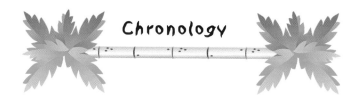

Chronology

(All dates BCE)

106 Marcus Tullius Cicero is born in Arpinum on January 3

90 Joins the military; serves in Social War

81 Starts career as an advocate

80 Defends Sextus Roscius Amerinus

79 Marries Terentia; leaves to study abroad in Athens and Rhodes; daughter Tullia born on August 5

77 Returns to Italy

75 Elected quaestor in Sicily and joins the Senate

70 Prosecutes Verres

69 Named aedile

66 Named praetor

65 Son Marcus is born

63 Elected consul; uncovers Catiline Conspiracy

58 Forced into exile; goes to Greece

55 Writes *De oratore* (On the Orator)

52 Begins writing *De legibus* (On the Laws)

51 Serves as proconsul, or governor, of Cilicia

47 Pardoned by Caesar; divorces Terentia

46 Marries Publilia

45 Tullia dies; divorces Publilia

43 Cicero is declared an enemy of the state and is executed on December 7

Timeline in History

BCE

211 Hannibal of Carthage (in North Africa) marches against Rome.

202 Hannibal is defeated by Scipio Africanus.

146 Carthage is destroyed; Greece becomes part of the Roman Empire.

100 Julius Caesar is born.

82 Sulla becomes Roman dictator.

73 Spartacus leads a Roman slave revolt.

63 Caesar's great-nephew Octavian is born. Catiline conspires to take over Rome.

60 First Triumvirate is formed by Caesar, Pompey, and Crassus.

49 Crassus dies; Pompey and Senate flee as Caesar's army approaches Rome.

48 Alexandria's great library is destroyed by fire. Caesar becomes Roman dictator.

44 Caesar is assassinated on the Ides of March (March 15).

43 The Second Triumverate is formed by Octavian, Marc Antony, and Marcus Lepidus.

40 The Roman Senate names Herod the Great king of Judea.

37 Marc Antony marries Cleopatra.

30 Antony and Cleopatra commit suicide after Octavian captures Alexandria.

27 Octavian is named Emperor Augustus, signifying the end of the Roman Republic.

19 Virgil, author of the *Aeneid* (which recounts the founding of Rome), dies.

8 Rome conducts a census that sends Mary and Joseph to Bethlehem, where Mary gives birth to Jesus.

CE

30 Jesus is crucified in Palestine, a province of Rome under the rule of Herod.

41 Caligula (Gaius Caesar), called the "mad emperor," is murdered.

Chapter Notes

Chapter 1   The Catiline Conspiracy

1. Cicero, *First Oration Against Catiline*, http://www.4literature.net/Cicero/First_Oration_Against_Catiline/2.html

2. Gaius Sallustius Crispus, *Conspiracy of Catiline,* translation by the Rev. John Selby Watson, New York: Harper & Brothers, 1867; online at http://www.forumromanum.org/literature/sallust/catilinae.html

3. Ancient History Sourcebook: "The Twelve Tables, c. 450 BCE" http://www.fordham.edu/halsall/ancient/12tables.html

4. Ibid.

Chapter 2   Setting His Sights

1. Anthony Everitt, *Cicero: The Life and Times of Rome's Greatest Politician* (New York: Random House, 2001), p. 21.

2. Ibid., p. 33.

Chapter 3   A Rising Star

1. Torsten Petersson, *Cicero: A Biography* (Berkeley: University of California Press, 1920), p. 74.

2. Cicero, *De re publica—De legibus,* with English translation by Clinton Walker Keyes (Cambridge/London: Harvard University Press [The Loeb Classical Library: Cicero, Vol. XVI (LCL 213)], 1994; online at http://www.gettysburgsem.org/studies/appendix1.htm

Chapter 4   Political Aspirations

1. Hannis Taylor, *Cicero: A Sketch of His Life and Works* (Chicago: A.C. McClurg, 1916), p. 202.

2. Cicero, *Select Letters to Several Friends,* "To Terentia, to My Dearest Tullia, and to My Son," April 30, [58 BCE], translated by W. Melmoth; online at http://www.4literature.net/Cicero/Select_Letters_to_Several_Friends/2.html

Chapter 5   Civil War

1. Cicero, *Select Letters to Several Friends,* "To Tiro," December [54 BCE], translated by W. Melmoth; online at http://www.4literature.net/Cicero/Select_Letters_to_Several_Friends/9.html

2. M. Tullius Cicero, *Orations: The Fourteen Orations Against Marcus Antonius (Philippics),* "The Fourth Oration . . . ," edited by C. D. Yonge. Based on the book by M. Tullius Cicero, *The Orations of Marcus Tullius Cicero,* literally translated by C. D. Yonge (London: George Bell & Sons, 1903), online at http://www.perseus.tufts.edu/cgi-bin/ptext?doc=Perseus%3Atext%3A1999.02.0021&query=head%3D%238

3. Plutarch, *Cicero,* translated by John Dryden, online at http://classics.mit.edu//Plutarch/cicero.html

4. Plutarch, *The Parallel Lives,* translated by Bernadotte Perrin, online at http://penelope.uchicago.edu/Thayer/E/Roman/Texts/Plutarch/Lives/Cicero*.html

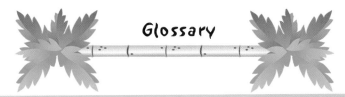
Glossary

advocate (AD-voh-ket)—a Roman attorney; advocates were not allowed to take money.

aedile (EE-dial)—an elected magistrate who oversaw city government.

Augustus (uh-GUS-tus)—a Latin term that means "majestic" or "venerable" and which came to be used to identify the Roman Emperor.

conscription (kon-SKRIP-shun)—a system of compulsory recruitment for the armed services; a draft.

consul (KON-sul)—one of two chief magistrates elected by the Senate for one-year terms. During the Republic, consuls were the supreme Roman leaders. After Caesar Augustus, the consuls were still the highest-ranking officials besides the emperor.

emperor (EM-peh-ror)—one who rules an empire. An emperor can inherit the position or can take it by military or political force.

extortion (ek-STOR-shun)—the illegal use of force or a position of authority to obtain money or valuables from someone.

litter (LIH-tur)—a seat or chair mounted between two poles that is carried by people holding the poles.

magistrate (MAA-jih-strayt)—a judge.

patricians (puh-TRIH-shins)—the Roman aristocrats; also, a member of one of Rome's original noble families.

plebeians (pluh-BEE-ans)—members of the Roman lower classes.

praetor (PREE-tor)—a high-level civil or military governor of a small province or large city; appointed for one-year terms, these Roman magistrates would be on par with a modern judge.

proconsul (proe-KON-sul)—provincial governors appointed by the Senate to rule outlying territories.

proscription (proe-SKRIP-shun)—naming someone an outlaw and condemning the person to death, with the property of the condemned taken by the government.

quaestor (KWEH-stir)—a financial officer who served as tax collector and was elected for one-year terms. Quaestors were automatically given a seat in the Senate.

rhetoric (REH-tor-ik)—the art of using language to persuade people.

senator (SEH-neh-tur)—a member of the Senate; seats were held by both plebeians and aristocrats. Anyone who served in a higher office—such as quaestor, praetor, or consul—was automatically given a seat in the Senate.

Further Reading

For Young Adults

Cicero, Marcus Tullius. *On the Good Life.* New York: Penguin Classics, 1971.

Forsyth, Fiona. *Cicero: Defender of the Republic. Leaders of Ancient Rome.* New York: Rosen Publishing Group, 2003.

Malam, John, and Mike Stuart Foster. *The Traveler's Guide to Ancient Rome.* New York: Scholastic, 2001.

Taylor, David. *Cicero and Rome. Inside the Ancient World.* Gloucestershire, UK: Nelson Thornes Ltd., 1982.

Works Consulted

Ancient History Sourcebook: "The Twelve Tables, c. 450 BCE" http://www.fordham.edu/halsall/ ancient/12tables.html

Cicero, M. Tullius. *Orations: The Fourteen Orations Against Marcus Antonius (Philippics).* Edited by C. D. Yonge. Based on the book: M. Tullius Cicero, *The Orations of Marcus Tullius Cicero,* literally translated by C. D. Yonge. London: George Bell & Sons, 1903. Online at http://www.perseus.tufts.edu/ cgi-bin/ptext?lookup=Cic.+Phil.+toc

Cicero. *First Oration Against Catiline.* http:// www.4literature.net/Cicero/ First_Oration_Against_Catiline/2.html

Cicero. *De re publica—De legibus.* With English translation by Clinton Walker Keyes. Cambridge/London: Harvard University Press (The Loeb Classical Library: Cicero, Vol. XVI (LCL 213), 1994. Online at http://www.gettysburgsem.org/studies/ appendix1.htm

Cicero. *Select Letters to Several Friends.* Translated by W. Melmoth. http://www.4literature.net/Cicero/ Select_Letters_to_Several_Friends/

Crispus, Gaius Sallustius. *Conspiracy of Catiline.* Translated by the Rev. John Selby Watson. New York: Harper & Brothers, 1867. Online at http://www.forumromanum.org/ literature/sallust/catilinae.html

Everitt, Anthony. *Cicero: The Life and Times of Rome's Greatest Politician.* New York: Random House, 2001.

Petersson, Torsten. *Cicero: A Biography.* Berkeley: University of California Press, 1920.

Plutarch. *Cicero.* Translated by John Dryden. Online at http://classics.mit.edu// Plutarch/cicero.html

Plutarch, *The Parallel Lives,* translated by Bernadotte Perrin. Online at http://penelope.uchicago.edu/Thayer/E/ Roman/Texts/Plutarch/Lives/ Cicero*.html

Taylor, Hannis, *Cicero: A Sketch of His Life and Works.* Chicago: A.C. McClurg, 1916.

On the Internet

An Online Encyclopedia of Roman Emperors http://www.roman-emperors.org/ impindex.htm

Cicero's Works http://www.4literature.net/Cicero/

The Internet Classics Archive http://classics.mit.edu//Plutarch/ cicero.html

Index